They are very smart.
They learn to use tools!

An Animal Family

APES AND BABIES

By Adelaide Redwood

Gareth Stevens PUBLISHING

Please visit our website, www.garethstevens.com. For a free color catalog of all our high-quality books, call toll free 1-800-542-2595 or fax 1-877-542-2596.

Cataloging-in-Publication Data

Names: Redwood, Adelaide.
Title: Apes and babies / Adelaide Redwood.
Description: New York : Gareth Stevens Publishing, 2018. | Series: An animal family | Includes index.
Identifiers: ISBN 9781482463651 (pbk.) | ISBN 9781482463675 (library bound) | ISBN 9781482463668 (6 pack)
Subjects: LCSH: Apes–Juvenile literature. | Apes–Infancy–Juvenile literature.
Classification: LCC QL737.P9 R43 2018 | DDC 599.8–dc23

First Edition

Published in 2018 by
Gareth Stevens Publishing
111 East 14th Street, Suite 349
New York, NY 10003

Editor: Ryan Nagelhout
Designer: Samantha DeMartin

Photo credits: Cover, pp. 1, 15, 17, 19 GODKOV ANDREY/Shutterstock.com; p. 5 Anna Kucherova/Shutterstock.com; pp. 7, 24 (tool) Kletr/Shutterstock.com; p. 9 Nick Fox/Shutterstock.com; pp. 11, 13 (bottom left) Sergey Uryadnikov/Shutterstock.com; p. 13 (top right) Eugene Kalenkovich/Shutterstock.com; p. 13 (bottom right) ForeverLee/Shutterstock.com; p. 13 (top right) FCG/Shutterstock.com; p. 21 Joca de Jong/Shutterstock.com; p. 23 Nagel Photography/Shutterstock.com; p. 24 (mountains) Travel Stock/Shutterstock.com; p. 24 (jungle) Ivanov Gleb/Shutterstock.com.

Printed in the United States of America

CPSIA compliance information: Batch #CS17GS: For further information contact Gareth Stevens, New York, New York at 1-800-542-2595.

Contents

Ape Fun 4
What's to Eat? 8
Apes All Over 12
Cute Babies 18
Words to Know 24
Index. 24

Apes are fun animals.

They eat plants and animals.

They like to live
in groups.
This is called a tribe.

They live
in many places.

Some live in jungles.

Others live
on mountains!

Ape babies are very cute.

Mothers take care of baby apes.

They give them milk.

Words to Know

jungle

mountains

tool

Index

apes 4, 18, 20

milk 22

plants 8

tribe 10